ROCK & ROLL CROSSWORDS

MUSICAL CROSSWORDS FOR ROCK 'N' ROLL LOVERS

@MOLLYMCMANUS

CHAPTER 1:

THE PIONEERS OF ROCK 'N' ROLL

DID YOU KNOW? ELVIS PRESLEY, OFTEN CALLED "THE KING OF ROCK 'N' ROLL," HELD THE RECORD FOR THE MOST SONGS CHARTING ON THE BILLBOARD HOT 100, WITH 149 CHARTING HITS, INCLUDING 18 NUMBER-ONE SINGLES. HIS INFLUENCE ON MUSIC AND CULTURE IS SO PROFOUND THAT HIS HOME, GRACELAND, IS THE SECOND MOST VISITED HOUSE IN THE UNITED STATES, AFTER THE WHITE HOUSE!

ELVIS PRESLEY: THE KING OF ROCK 'N' ROLL

ACROSS

2. BRANCH OF THE MILITARY ELVIS SERVED IN

5. ELVIS'S BIRTHPLACE IN MISSISSIPPI

8. FIRST WORD OF A FAMOUS ELVIS SONG ABOUT JEALOUSY

9. GENRE OF MUSIC ELVIS LOVED AND RECORDED EXTENSIVELY

DOWN

1. CITY WHERE ELVIS HAD A LONG-STANDING PERFORMANCE RESIDENCY

3. CITY WHERE ELVIS RECORDED HIS FIRST SONG

4. PART OF THE BODY ELVIS FAMOUSLY MOVED WHILE PERFORMING

6. ELVIS'S FAMOUS MANSION

7. FIRST WORD OF ELVIS'S HIT SONG ABOUT A DOG

10. RECORD LABEL WHERE ELVIS BEGAN HIS CAREER

CHUCK BERRY: THE GUITAR LEGEND

ACROSS

1. CHUCK BERRY'S SIGNATURE STAGE MOVE
4. FIRST WORD OF A BERRY SONG URGING BEETHOVEN TO HEAR ROCK 'N' ROLL
5. PLACE WHERE CHUCK BERRY SPENT TIME THAT INFLUENCED HIS SONGWRITING
7. CHUCK BERRY'S FIRST BIG HIT
9. RECORD LABEL THAT RELEASED MOST OF CHUCK BERRY'S HITS
10. TITLE OF A CHUCK BERRY SONG ABOUT LOOKING FOR A WOMAN

DOWN

2. CITY WHERE CHUCK BERRY PERFORMED FOR THE OPENING OF THE ROCK & ROLL HALL OF FAME
3. BRAND OF GUITAR CHUCK BERRY FAMOUSLY PLAYED
6. CHUCK BERRY'S HOMETOWN (TWO WORDS, ONE ANSWER)
8. FIRST NAME OF THE CHARACTER IN "JOHNNY B.GOODE"

BUDDY HOLLY: THE CRICKETS AND THE CLASSICS

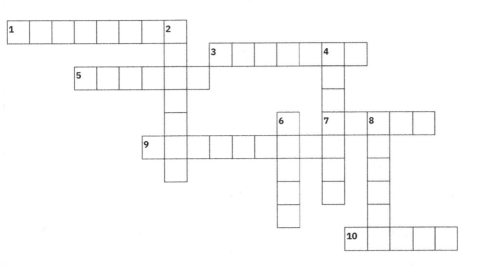

ACROSS

1. THE SOUND ASSOCIATED WITH BUDDY HOLLY'S AND, THE CRICKETS

3. TEXAS CITY WHERE BUDDY HOLLY WAS BORN

5. FIRST NAME OF THE PRODUCER WHO WORKED WITH BUDDY HOLLY ON MANY HITS

7. MODE OF TRANSPORTATION IN WHICH BUDDY HOLLY TRAGICALLY DIED

9. TITLE OF ONE OF BUDDY HOLLY'S SONGS ABOUT LOVE

10. BUDDY'S LAST NAME AND STAGE NAME

DOWN

2. ICONIC ACCESSORY BUDDY HOLLY WAS KNOWN FOR WEARING

4. LAST NAME OF THE GUITARIST INFLUENCED BY BUDDY HOLLY

6. FIRST NAME OF BUDDY HOLLY'S FAMOUS LOVE SONG (E.G., "PEGGY SUE")

8. THEATER WHERE BUDDY HOLLY BROKE RACIAL BARRIERS BY PERFORMING

PAGE 35

FATS DOMINO: THE NEW ORLEANS SOUND

ACROSS

4. FATS DOMINO WAS A PART OF THIS CULTURAL GROUP FROM LOUISIANA

5. FATS DOMINO'S SONG THAT SAYS "I'M WALKING TO NEW ORLEANS"

8. FATS'S LAST NAME, WHICH BECAME HIS STAGE NAME

9. RECORD LABEL WHERE FATS DOMINO RELEASED MANY OF HIS HITS

10. THE WARD IN NEW ORLEANS WHERE FATS DOMINO GREW UP (AS IN "NINTH WARD")

DOWN

1. INSTRUMENT FATS DOMINO PLAYED IN A BOOGIE-WOOGIE STYLE

2. FIRST WORD OF A FATS DOMINO SONG ABOUT A HILL

3. FIRST WORD OF THE FAMOUS NEW ORLEANS FESTIVAL FATS OFTEN PLAYED (AS IN "MARDI GRAS")

6. FIRST WORD OF A FATS DOMINO SONG TITLED "AIN'T THAT A SHAME"

7. FIRST PART OF FATS DOMINO'S NICKNAME

PAGE 36

6

LITTLE RICHARD: THE ARCHITECT OF ROCK

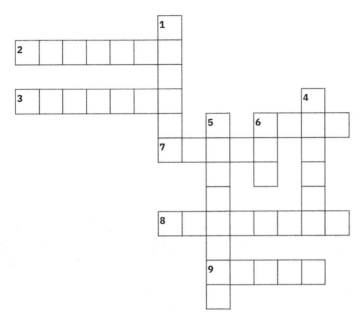

ACROSS

2. U.S. STATE WHERE LITTLE RICHARD WAS BORN

3. TITLE OF A LITTLE RICHARD HIT ABOUT A GIRL LEAVING HIM

6. ANOTHER REPEATED SYLLABLE IN "TUTTI FRUTTI" (THIRD PART OF "AWOPBOPALOOBOP")

7. INSTRUMENT LITTLE RICHARD PLAYED WITH FLAMBOYANT STYLE

8. LITTLE RICHARD'S OCCUPATION AFTER HE TEMPORARILY LEFT ROCK 'N' ROLL

9. FIRST WORD OF A LITTLE RICHARD HIT SONG WITH A LOT OF "AWOPBOPALOOBOP" ENERGY

DOWN

1. LITTLE RICHARD WAS KNOWN FOR WEARING THIS ON STAGE, BREAKING NORMS

4. DANCE STYLE LITTLE RICHARD HELPED POPULARIZE

5. VOCAL STYLE LITTLE RICHARD OFTEN USED IN HIS SINGING

6. REPEATED SYLLABLE IN "TUTTI FRUTTI" (SECOND PART OF "AWOPBOPALOOBOP")

PAGE 37

7

CHAPTER 2:

ICONIC ROCK SONGS

DID YOU KNOW? THE 1960S PRODUCED SOME OF THE MOST ICONIC ROCK ANTHEMS EVER, WITH MANY SONGS FROM THIS ERA REMAINING TIMELESS CLASSICS. THE ROLLING STONES' "SATISFACTION" WAS SO INFLUENTIAL THAT IT BECAME THE BAND'S FIRST U.S. NUMBER-ONE HIT, AND IT'S CONSIDERED ONE OF THE GREATEST ROCK SONGS OF ALL TIME. THIS ERA OF MUSIC SET THE STAGE FOR COUNTLESS ARTISTS AND GENRES THAT FOLLOWED!

TOP 10 HITS OF THE 1950S

PAGE 38

ACROSS

2. BOOM SONG BY THE CHORDS THAT IS CONSIDERED ONE OF THE FIRST ROCK 'N' ROLL HITS

6. FIRST WORD OF "GREAT BALLS OF FIRE" SINGER'S LAST NAME

7. FIRST TWO WORDS OF A HIT BY BILL HALEY & HIS COMETS (AS IN "ROCK AROUND THE CLOCK")

9. FIRST WORD OF ELVIS'S BALLAD ABOUT BEING LONELY AT CHRISTMAS

10. FIRST NAME OF THE ARTIST WHO SANG "LA BAMBA"

DOWN

1. GROUP THAT SANG "THE GREAT PRETENDER"

3. SONG BY JIMMIE RODGERS THAT HIT #1 IN 1957

4. FIRST WORD OF ELVIS'S 1956 HIT ABOUT A HOTEL

5. LAST WORD OF "HEART AND SOUL" GROUP THE FOUR _____

8. FIRST WORD OF LITTLE RICHARD'S BREAKOUT HIT SONG

1960S ROCK ANTHEMS

PAGE 39

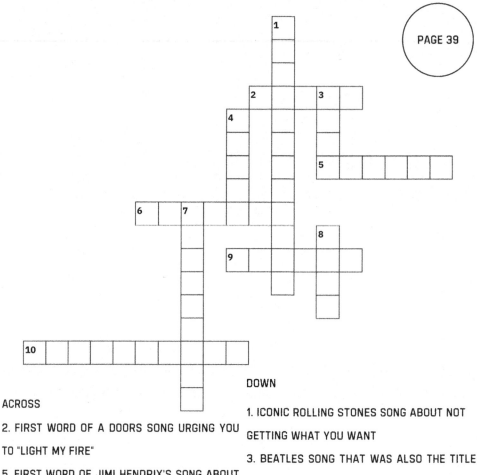

DOWN

ACROSS

2. FIRST WORD OF A DOORS SONG URGING YOU TO "LIGHT MY FIRE"

5. FIRST WORD OF JIMI HENDRIX'S SONG ABOUT A HAZE

6. ARETHA FRANKLIN'S ANTHEM DEMANDING THIS

9. FIRST WORD OF JIMI HENDRIX'S SONG WITH THE WORD "CHILD" IN THE TITLE

10. LAST WORD IN THE TITLE OF BOB DYLAN'S SONG "MR. _____ MAN"

1. ICONIC ROLLING STONES SONG ABOUT NOT GETTING WHAT YOU WANT

3. BEATLES SONG THAT WAS ALSO THE TITLE OF A MOVIE

4. FIRST WORD OF "HOUSE OF THE RISING SUN" BY THE ANIMALS

7. LAST WORD OF A COLORFUL BEATLES SONG

8. FIRST WORD OF THE BEACH BOYS' HIT ABOUT GOOD VIBRATIONS

ROCK BALLADS: THE SOFTER SIDE

ACROSS

. BEATLES' MOST COVERED BALLAD

. FIRST WORD OF THE RIGHTEOUS BROTHERS'

IT ABOUT LOVE (AS IN "UNCHAINED MELODY")

. FIRST WORD OF THE EVERLY BROTHERS' HIT

BOUT DREAMING

. BEE GEES BALLAD THAT SAID "IT'S ONLY

_____. AND WORDS ARE ALL I HAVE"

. BEATLES SONG WITH A GIRL'S NAME AS THE

ITLE

. ROLLING STONES' BALLAD ABOUT A

YSTERIOUS WOMAN

DOWN

1. SONG BY THE BEATLES THAT'S BEEN

COVERED

BY OVER 2,200 ARTISTS

4. FIRST WORD OF THE SIMON & GARFUNKEL

HIT

"BRIDGE OVER TROUBLED WATER"

6. ROY ORBISON'S TEARFUL BALLAD

7. LAST WORD OF "WHAT KIND OF FOOL AM I" BY

SAMMY DAVIS JR.

PAGE 40

SONGS THAT SHAPED ROCK HISTORY

PAGE 41

12

ACROSS

2. FIRST WORD OF THE BEATLES' SONG "HEY JUDE"

6. JOHN LENNON'S SONG ABOUT PEACE AND HOPE

7. FIRST WORD OF A QUEEN SONG WITH A RHAPSODIC TITLE

10. LAST WORD IN THE NAME OF THE BAND THAT SANG "COMFORTABLY NUMB" (AS IN "PINK FLOYD")

DOWN

1. LAST WORD IN THE NAME OF THE BAND THAT SANG "WHOLE LOTTA LOVE" (AS IN "LED ZEPPELIN")

3. DAVID BOWIE'S ANTHEM ABOUT OVERCOMING THE ODDS

4. FIRST WORD OF A LED ZEPPELIN CLASSIC ABOUT A JOURNEY TO HEAVEN

5. BEATLES SONG ABOUT A BIRD WITH BROKEN WINGS

8. FIRST WORD OF AN EAGLES SONG ABOUT A CALIFORNIA ESTABLISHMENT

9. FIRST WORD OF A BRUCE SPRINGSTEEN HIT ABOUT LIFE IN THE USA

DANCE CRAZE HITS

PAGE 42

ACROSS

3. LITTLE EVA'S HIT SONG AND DANCE 6. FIRST WORD OF A DANCE BY THE OLYMPICS (AS IN "HULLY GULLY")

7. DANCE MOVE MENTIONED IN "SWIM" BY BOBBY FREEMAN

8. DANCE POPULARIZED IN THE 1950S, OFTEN DONE TO ROCK 'N' ROLL

9. DANCE MENTIONED IN THE SONG "THE FRUG" BY THE FRANTICS

DOWN

1. DANCE POPULARIZED BY THE ORLONS 2. DANCE MADE FAMOUS BY CHUBBY CHECKER AFTER "THE TWIST"

4. FIRST WORD OF A DANCE CRAZE NAMED AFTER POTATOES (AS IN "MASHED POTATO")

5. DANCE MADE FAMOUS BY CHUBBY CHECKER

8. DANCE MENTIONED IN "THE JERK" BY THE LARKS

CHAPTER 3:

THE BRITISH

INVASION

DID YOU KNOW? THE BRITISH INVASION REVOLUTIONIZED ROCK 'N' ROLL, WITH BANDS LIKE THE BEATLES AND THE ROLLING STONES LEADING THE CHARGE. THE BEATLES HOLD THE RECORD FOR THE MOST NUMBER-ONE HITS ON THE BILLBOARD HOT 100, WITH 20 CHART-TOPPERS! THEIR INNOVATIVE APPROACH TO SONGWRITING, RECORDING, AND PERFORMING RESHAPED POPULAR MUSIC AND CULTURE, INFLUENCING COUNTLESS ARTISTS ACROSS THE GLOBE.

THE BEATLES

ACROSS

1. THE HAIRSTYLE FAMOUSLY ASSOCIATED WITH THE BEATLES (AS IN "MOP TOP")

4. BEATLES' SONG AND MOVIE TITLE ASKING FOR ASSISTANCE

7. ANIMAL REFERENCED IN THE BEATLES' SONG "I AM THE _____"

8. FIRST NAME OF JOHN LENNON'S WIFE

9. FIRST NAME OF THE BEATLES' DRUMMER

10. FIRST WORD OF THE BEATLES' FAMOUS STUDIO AND ALBUM (AS IN "ABBEY ROAD")

DOWN

2. FIRST WORD IN THE ALBUM TITLE "SGT. PEPPER'S LONELY HEARTS CLUB BAND"

3. THE BEATLES' HOMETOWN IN ENGLAND

5. FIRST NAME OF THE CHARACTER IN "ELEANOR RIGBY"

6. ONE-WORD TITLE OF A BEATLES BALLAD ABOUT NOSTALGIA

PAGE 43

THE WHO: ROCK OPERA REVOLUTIONARIES

ACROSS

2. THE WHO'S SONG ABOUT BEING A REPLACEMENT

3. TITLE OF THE WHO'S ROCK OPERA ABOUT A DEAF, DUMB, AND BLIND BOY

7. THE WHO'S ANTHEM DECLARING "HOPE I DIE BEFORE I GET OLD" (TWO WORDS, ONE ANSWER)

8. BAND NAME FOLLOWED BY THE WORDS "ARE YOU" IN A FAMOUS SONG

9. LAST NAME REFERENCED IN "BABA O'RILEY" (COMMONLY MISTAKEN AS "TEENAGE WASTELAND")

DOWN

1. THE WHO'S ROCK OPERA ABOUT MODS AND ROCKERS

4. FIRST NAME OF THE WHO'S LEAD SINGER DALTREY

5. FIRST NAME OF THE WHO'S GUITARIST TOWNSHEND

6. GAME REFERENCED IN THE WHO'S "PINBALL WIZARD"

7. LAST NAME OF THE WHO'S DRUMMER KEITH

16

PAGE 44

THE ROLLING STONES: ROCK'S BAD BOYS

ACROSS

1. FIRST WORD OF THE ROLLING STONES' SONG "RUBY TUESDAY"

4. LAST NAME OF THE ROLLING STONES' LEAD SINGER

5. LAST NAME OF THE ROLLING STONES' ORIGINAL MEMBER BRIAN

6. FIRST WORD OF THE ROLLING STONES ALBUM "STICKY FINGERS"

7. FIRST WORD OF THE ALBUM TITLE "TATTOO YOU"

8. FIRST NAME OF THE ROLLING STONES' GUITARIST RICHARDS

9. ROLLING STONES BALLAD ABOUT A MYSTERIOUS WOMAN

DOWN

2. FIRST WORD OF THE ROLLING STONES ALBUM "BEGGARS BANQUET"

3. ROLLING STONES HIT SONG ABOUT NOT GETTING WHAT YOU WANT

10. FIRST WORD OF THE ROLLING STONES SONG ABOUT SHELTER

PAGE 45

THE KINKS: THE BRITISH SOUND

ACROSS

4. FIRST WORD OF THE KINKS' ALBUM "THE VILLAGE GREEN PRESERVATION SOCIETY"

5. FIRST WORD OF THE KINKS' SONG ABOUT PICTURES IN A GALLERY

8. FIRST WORD OF THE KINKS' SONG ABOUT A CERTAIN AFTERNOON

9. TITLE OF THE KINKS' ALBUM SUBTITLED "OR

THE DECLINE AND FALL OF THE BRITISH EMPIRE"

10. THE KINKS' SONG ABOUT A GIRL WHO ISN'T

QUITE WHAT SHE SEEMS

DOWN

1. FIRST WORD OF THE KINKS' HIT ABOUT BEING "TIRED OF WAITING FOR YOU"

2. LAST NAME OF THE KINKS' CO-FOUNDER AND GUITARIST DAVE

3. THE KINKS SONG WHERE LOLA REAPPEARS

6. FIRST NAME OF THE KINKS' LEAD SINGER DAVIES

7. FIRST WORD OF THE KINKS' HIT SONG ABOUT A SUNSET

PAGE 46

18

THE YARDBIRDS AND BEYOND: GUITAR GODS

ACROSS

1. BAND CLAPTON FORMED AFTER LEAVING THE YARDBIRDS

4. FIRST WORD OF THE YARDBIRDS' HIT SONG "SHAPES OF THINGS"

7. YARDBIRDS' HIT SONG THAT CLAPTON DISLIKED (THREE WORDS, ONE ANSWER)

9. LAST NAME OF THE BAND PAGE FORMED AFTER THE YARDBIRDS (AS IN "LED ZEPPELIN")

10. LAST NAME OF THE GUITARIST WHO FOLLOWED CLAPTON IN THE YARDBIRDS

DOWN

2. FIRST WORD OF THE YARDBIRDS' ALBUM "RAVE UP"

3. LAST NAME OF THE GUITARIST NICKNAMED "SLOWHAND"

5. LAST NAME OF THE GUITARIST WHO LATER FORMED LED ZEPPELIN

6. FIRST WORD OF THE YARDBIRDS' SONG "TRAIN KEPT A-ROLLIN'"

8. FIRST NAME OF THE YARDBIRDS' BASSIST MCCARTY

PAGE

47

CHAPTER 4:

ROCK 'N' ROLL IN POP CULTURE

DID YOU KNOW? THE INFLUENCE OF ROCK 'N' ROLL EXTENDS FAR BEYOND JUST MUSIC—ITS IMPACT ON FASHION, TELEVISION, MOVIES, AND EVEN ADVERTISING HAS BEEN IMMENSE. THE BEATLES' APPEARANCE ON "THE ED SULLIVAN SHOW" IN 1964 WAS WATCHED BY A RECORD-BREAKING 73 MILLION VIEWERS, SOLIDIFYING ROCK 'N' ROLL AS A CENTRAL PART OF GLOBAL POP CULTURE AND USHERING IN THE BRITISH INVASION. ROCK 'N' ROLL WASN'T JUST MUSIC; IT WAS A CULTURAL REVOLUTION!

FASHION IN ROCK: LEATHER JACKETS TO MINI SKIRTS

ACROSS

3. TYPE OF SOCKS POPULAR IN THE 1950S ROCK 'N' ROLL ERA

5. TYPE OF SHOE WITH A THICK SOLE AND LOW HEEL, POPULAR IN THE 1950S

7. HAIRSTYLE MADE FAMOUS BY ELVIS PRESLEY

9. BRITISH YOUTH SUBCULTURE KNOWN FOR THEIR DRAPE JACKETS AND ROCK 'N' ROLL STYLE (AS IN "TEDDY BOYS")

10. FABRIC ASSOCIATED WITH ROCK 'N' ROLL FASHION, ESPECIALLY JEANS

DOWN

1. TERM FOR THE LEATHER JACKET-WEARING ROCK 'N' ROLL REBELS OF THE 1950S

2. MATERIAL ASSOCIATED WITH THE REBELLIOUS ROCK 'N' ROLL LOOK

4. VOLUMINOUS HAIRSTYLE POPULAR AMONG WOMEN IN THE 1960S

6. TYPE OF SKIRT THAT BECAME A SYMBOL OF 1950S ROCK 'N' ROLL FASHION

8. 1960S BRITISH SUBCULTURE KNOWN FOR ITS

SHARP FASHION AND LOVE OF ROCK 'N' ROLL

PAGE 48

21

ROCK 'N' ROLL HALL OF FAME: THE EARLY INDUCTEES

PAGE 49

ACROSS

4. LAST NAME OF THE SINGER AND PIANIST KNOWN FOR BLENDING SOUL AND ROCK 'N' ROLL

5. LAST NAME OF THE ROCK 'N' ROLL INNOVATOR KNOWN FOR HIS DISTINCTIVE BEAT AND GUITAR STYLE

6. LAST NAME OF THE SINGER KNOWN FOR "YOU SEND ME" AND A KEY FIGURE IN THE DEVELOPMENT OF SOUL AND ROCK 8. LAST NAME OF THE "PEGGY SUE" SINGER INDUCTED IN 1986

10. LAST NAME OF THE "QUEEN OF SOUL" WHO WAS ALSO AN EARLY INDUCTEE

DOWN

1. LAST NAME OF "TUTTI FRUTTI" ROCK 'N' ROLL PIONEER INDUCTED EARLY

2. FIRST INDUCTEE INTO THE ROCK 'N' ROLL HALL OF FAME

3. LAST NAME OF THE "ROLL OVER BEETHOVEN" SINGER INDUCTED INTO THE HALL OF FAME

7. LAST NAME OF THE BROTHERS WHO WERE EARLY INDUCTEES

9. LAST NAME OF THE "GREAT BALLS OF FIRE" SINGER INDUCTED INTO THE HALL OF FAME

TV SHOWS AND ROCK PERFORMANCES

ACROSS

. ROCK 'N' ROLL STAR WHO FAMOUSLY PPEARED ON "THE ED SULLIVAN SHOW" IN 956

. TV SHOW ABOUT A FICTIONAL ROCK BAND, EADING TO REAL CHART-TOPPING HITS

. TV SHOW THAT, WHILE FOCUSED ON SOUL, LSO FEATURED ROCK 'N' ROLL CROSSOVERS TWO WORDS, ONE ANSWER)

. POPULAR TV SHOW HOSTED BY DICK CLARK HAT FEATURED ROCK 'N' ROLL ACTS (TWO VORDS, ONE ANSWER)

. BRITISH TV SHOW THAT SHOWCASED ROCK '

OLL HITS (THREE WORDS, ONE ANSWER)

8. TV SHOW WHERE THE BEATLES MADE THEIR .S. DEBUT (TWO WORDS, ONE ANSWER)

DOWN

1. 1970S TV SHOW THAT FEATURED LIVE ROCK PERFORMANCES (TWO WORDS, ONE ANSWER)

2. 1960S NBC TV SHOW KNOWN FOR SHOWCASING ROCK 'N' ROLL STARS

4. 1960S AMERICAN MUSIC TV SHOW THAT FEATURED ROCK 'N' ROLL PERFORMANCES

7. BAND THAT CAUSED "BEATLEMANIA" AFTER THEIR ED SULLIVAN PERFORMANCE

PAGE 50

23

ROCK 'N' ROLL MOVIES: THE SOUNDTRACKS OF A GENERATION

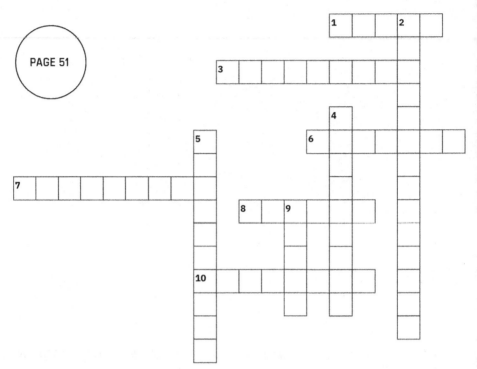

PAGE 51

ACROSS

1. FIRST WORD OF THE TITLE "DIRTY DANCING," SET IN THE 1960S

3. 1984 MOVIE ABOUT A TOWN THAT BANS DANCING

6. MOVIE ABOUT THE LIFE OF RITCHIE VALENS (TWO WORDS, ONE ANSWER)

7. FIRST WORD OF THE ELVIS MOVIE AND SONG "JAILHOUSE ROCK"

8. 1978 MOVIE FEATURING A 1950S ROCK 'N' ROLL HIGH SCHOOL SETTING

10. FIRST WORD OF "AMERICAN GRAFFITI," A FILM SET IN THE EARLY 1960S

DOWN

2. MOVIE ABOUT AN IRISH SOUL BAND COVERING (60S HITS (TWO WORDS, ONE ANSWER)

4. MOVIE ABOUT A DANCE SHOW AND CIVIL RIGHTS SET IN THE 1960S

5. FIRST TWO WORDS OF THE JERRY LEE LEWIS BIOPIC TITLE (AS IN "GREAT BALLS OF FIRE!")

9. ROCK 'N' ROLL STAR WHO HAD A SUCCESSFUL FILM CAREER IN THE 1950S AND 1960S

ROCK 'N' ROLL IN ADVERTISING: THE SOUND OF SALES

ACROSS

2. INSTRUMENT OFTEN FEATURED IN ADS FOR ROCK 'N' ROLL-THEMED PRODUCTS

3. SOFT DRINK COMPANY THAT FAMOUSLY USED ROCK MUSIC IN ITS MARKETING, INCLUDING MICHAEL JACKSON

5. BEVERAGE COMPANY KNOWN FOR USING ROCK 'N' ROLL MUSIC IN THEIR ADS (TWO WORDS, ONE ANSWER)

9. BAND WHOSE SONG "REVOLUTION" WAS USED IN A NIKE COMMERCIAL

10. FASHION ITEM OFTEN SOLD USING ROCK 'N' ROLL IMAGERY AND MUSIC

DOWN

1. CAR BRAND THAT USED LED ZEPPELIN'S "ROCK AND ROLL" IN COMMERCIALS

4. APPLE PRODUCT THAT FEATURED VARIOUS ROCK 'N' ROLL SONGS IN ITS ADS

6. COMPANY THAT USED U2'S SONG "VERTIGO" IN AN AD CAMPAIGN

7. CAR COMPANY THAT USED THE WHO'S "BABA O'RILEY" IN A COMMERCIAL

8. NETWORK THAT REVOLUTIONIZED MUSIC ADVERTISING WITH ROCK 'N' ROLL MUSIC VIDEOS

PAGE 52

CHAPTER 5:

ROCK LEGENDS AND THEIR LEGACY

DID YOU KNOW? DESPITE THE PASSAGE OF TIME, MANY ROCK LEGENDS CONTINUE TO INFLUENCE NEW GENERATIONS OF MUSICIANS. ARTISTS LIKE PAUL MCCARTNEY AND THE ROLLING STONES' MICK JAGGER ARE STILL ACTIVELY TOURING AND CREATING MUSIC DECADES AFTER THEIR CAREERS BEGAN. THEIR ABILITY TO EVOLVE AND ADAPT WHILE STAYING TRUE TO THEIR ROCK 'N' ROLL ROOTS HAS ENSURED THEIR LEGACY ENDURES ACROSS THE AGES. ROCK 'N' ROLL TRULY IS TIMELESS!

SURVIVORS OF ROCK: ARTISTS WHO ENDURED

ACROSS

1. LAST NAME OF THE FLEETWOOD MAC SINGER STILL PERFORMING SOLO AND WITH THE BAND

6. LAST NAME OF THE GUITARIST KNOWN AS "SLOWHAND," WHO HAS HAD A LONG CAREER

7. LAST NAME OF THE AEROSMITH FRONTMAN KNOWN FOR HIS ENERGETIC PERFORMANCES

8. LAST NAME OF THE ROLLING STONES' GUITARIST KNOWN FOR HIS RESILIENCE

9. LAST NAME OF "THE BOSS" WHO IS FAMOUS FOR HIS LONG CONCERTS

10. LAST NAME OF THE FOLK-ROCK ICON STILL ACTIVE AFTER SIX DECADES

DOWN

2. LAST NAME OF THE RASPY-VOICED ROCKER KNOWN FOR "MAGGIE MAY"

3. LAST NAME OF THE WHO'S GUITARIST WHO HELPED PIONEER ROCK OPERAS

4. LAST NAME OF THE ROLLING STONES' LEAD SINGER WHO STILL TOURS

5. LAST NAME OF THE BEATLE WHO CONTINUES TO PERFORM GLOBALLY

PAGE 53

REUNIONS AND COMEBACKS: ROCK'S GREATEST RETURNS

PAGE 54

ACROSS

3. BAND THAT REUNITED IN 2007 FOR A WORLD
TOUR AFTER DECADES APART
5. BAND THAT FAMOUSLY SAID "HELL FREEZES OVER" AND THEN REUNITED
6. BAND THAT REUNITED WITH DAVID LEE ROTH
FOR TOURS IN THE 2000S
8. LAST NAME OF THE "BRIDGE OVER TROUBLED
WATER" SINGER WHO REUNITED WITH GARFUNKEL
10. LAST NAME OF THE "RED ROCKER" WHO REJOINED VAN HALEN IN 2004

DOWN

1. LAST NAME OF THE DRUMMER WHOSE BAND REUNITED FOR "THE DANCE"
2. LAST NAME OF THE GENESIS DRUMMER AND SINGER WHO RETURNED FOR A 2007 TOUR
4. BAND THAT HAS HAD MULTIPLE REUNIONS AND LINE-UP CHANGES, STAYING STRONG
7. BAND KNOWN FOR SURVIVING THE DEATH OF ITS LEAD SINGER AND COMING BACK STRONGER
9. LAST NAME OF THE LED ZEPPELIN GUITARIST WHO REUNITED WITH THE BAND IN 2007

28

ROCK 'N' ROLL'S ENDURING INFLUENCE: FROM THEN TO NOW

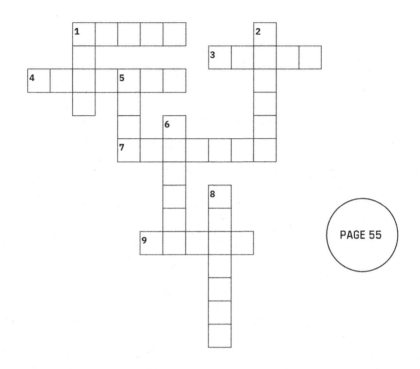

PAGE 55

ACROSS

LAST NAME OF THE GUITARIST AND SINGER
WHO DRAWS HEAVILY FROM BLUES-ROCK

. LAST NAME OF THE FOO FIGHTERS
FRONTMAN WHO STARTED AS NIRVANA'S
DRUMMER

. BAND THAT BROUGHT BACK GARAGE ROCK

THE EARLY 2000S, INSPIRED BY THE 1970S

. LAST NAME OF THE BRITISH SINGER-
SONGWRITER WHO OFTEN COVERS CLASSIC
ROCK SONGS

. LAST NAME OF THE COUNTRY SINGER WHO
INCORPORATES ROCK INTO HIS MUSIC

DOWN

1. LAST NAME OF THE POP STAR WHO
CHANNELS
ROCK, FUNK, AND SOUL IN HIS PERFORMANCES

2. LAST NAME OF THE NIRVANA FRONTMAN WHO
CITED THE BEATLES AS AN INFLUENCE

5. LAST NAME OF THE SINGER ALICIA, WHO WAS
INFLUENCED BY SOUL AND ROCK

6. LAST NAME OF THE PEARL JAM SINGER
INFLUENCED BY THE WHO

8. LAST NAME OF THE SINGER WHO BLENDS
ROCK, FUNK, AND SOUL INFLUENCES

COVER VERSIONS: NEW TAKES ON CLASSIC HITS

PAGE 56

DOWN

1. LAST NAME OF THE ARTIST WHO COVERED "BLUE SUEDE SHOES"

2. LAST NAME OF THE GUITARIST WHO COVERED

"I SHOT THE SHERIFF"

3. LAST NAME OF THE WHITE STRIPES FRONTMAN WHO COVERED "JOLENE"

7. LAST NAME OF THE SINGER WHO COVERED "BECAUSE THE NIGHT" AND CO-WROTE IT WITH SPRINGSTEEN

8. LAST NAME OF THE SINGER WHO FAMOUSLY COVERED "WITH A LITTLE HELP FROM MY FRIENDS"

ACROSS

3. LAST NAME OF THE SINGER WHO COVERED "VALERIE," MAKING IT A HIT

4. LAST NAME OF THE SINGER WHO MADE "ME AND BOBBY MCGEE" FAMOUS

5. LAST NAME OF THE GUITARIST WHO FAMOUSLY COVERED "ALL ALONG THE WATCHTOWER"

6. BAND THAT COVERED "CALIFORNIA SUN" AND

BROUGHT PUNK TO THE MASSES

8. LAST NAME OF THE COUNTRY ICON WHO COVERED NINE INCH NAILS' "HURT"

THE DAY THE MUSIC DIED: REMEMBERING THE LOST LEGENDS

ACROSS

2. LAST NAME OF "THE KING" WHO PASSED AWAY IN 1977

5. LAST NAME OF THE "OH, PRETTY WOMAN" SINGER WHO PASSED IN 1988

7. LAST NAME OF "THE BIG BOPPER," WHO WAS ON THE SAME ILL-FATED FLIGHT

8. LAST NAME OF THE GUITARIST FROM THE ALLMAN BROTHERS BAND WHO DIED IN 1971

9. LAST NAME OF THE "LA BAMBA" SINGER WHO ALSO PERISHED IN THE CRASH

10. LAST NAME OF THE FORMER BEATLE TRAGICALLY KILLED IN 1980

DOWN

1. LAST NAME OF THE LEGENDARY GUITARIST WHO ALSO DIED AT AGE 27

3. LAST NAME OF THE DOORS' LEAD SINGER WHO DIED AT AGE 27

4. LAST NAME OF THE SINGER WHO DIED IN A 1959 PLANE CRASH, KNOWN FOR "PEGGY SUE"

6. LAST NAME OF THE "PIECE OF MY HEART" SINGER WHO DIED IN 1970

PAGE 57

CHAPTER 6:

ANSWERS

ELVIS PRESLEY: THE KING OF ROCK 'N' ROLL

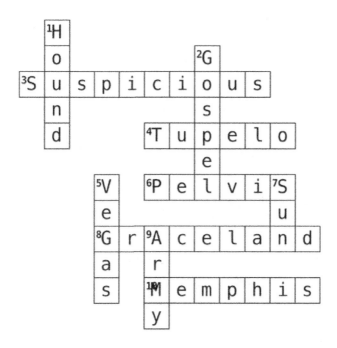

<table>
<tr><td></td><td>¹H</td><td></td><td></td><td></td><td></td><td></td></tr>
</table>

ACROSS

2. BRANCH OF THE MILITARY ELVIS SERVED IN

5. ELVIS'S BIRTHPLACE IN MISSISSIPPI

8. FIRST WORD OF A FAMOUS ELVIS SONG ABOUT JEALOUSY

9. GENRE OF MUSIC ELVIS LOVED AND RECORDED EXTENSIVELY

DOWN

1. CITY WHERE ELVIS HAD A LONG-STANDING PERFORMANCE RESIDENCY

3. CITY WHERE ELVIS RECORDED HIS FIRST SONG

4. PART OF THE BODY ELVIS FAMOUSLY MOVED WHILE PERFORMING

6. ELVIS'S FAMOUS MANSION

7. FIRST WORD OF ELVIS'S HIT SONG ABOUT A DOG

10. RECORD LABEL WHERE ELVIS BEGAN HIS CAREER

CHUCK BERRY: THE GUITAR LEGEND

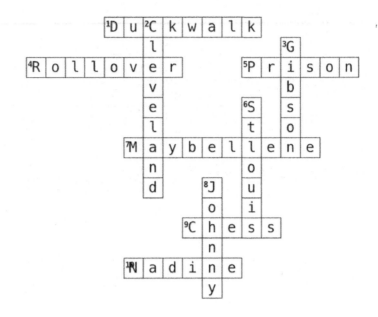

ACROSS

1. CHUCK BERRY'S SIGNATURE STAGE MOVE

4. FIRST WORD OF A BERRY SONG URGING BEETHOVEN TO HEAR ROCK 'N' ROLL

5. PLACE WHERE CHUCK BERRY SPENT TIME THAT INFLUENCED HIS SONGWRITING

7. CHUCK BERRY'S FIRST BIG HIT

9. RECORD LABEL THAT RELEASED MOST OF CHUCK BERRY'S HITS

10. TITLE OF A CHUCK BERRY SONG ABOUT LOOKING FOR A WOMAN

DOWN

2. CITY WHERE CHUCK BERRY PERFORMED FOR THE OPENING OF THE ROCK & ROLL HALL OF FAME

3. BRAND OF GUITAR CHUCK BERRY FAMOUSLY PLAYED

6. CHUCK BERRY'S HOMETOWN (TWO WORDS, ONE ANSWER)

8. FIRST NAME OF THE CHARACTER IN "JOHNNY B.GOODE"

BUDDY HOLLY: THE CRICKETS AND THE CLASSICS

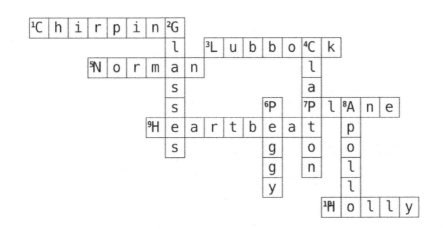

ACROSS

THE SOUND ASSOCIATED WITH BUDDY HOLLY'S

AND, THE CRICKETS

TEXAS CITY WHERE BUDDY HOLLY WAS BORN

FIRST NAME OF THE PRODUCER WHO WORKED WITH BUDDY HOLLY ON MANY HITS

MODE OF TRANSPORTATION IN WHICH BUDDY HOLLY TRAGICALLY DIED

TITLE OF ONE OF BUDDY HOLLY'S SONGS ABOUT LOVE

BUDDY'S LAST NAME AND STAGE NAME

DOWN

2. ICONIC ACCESSORY BUDDY HOLLY WAS KNOWN FOR WEARING

4. LAST NAME OF THE GUITARIST INFLUENCED BY BUDDY HOLLY

6. FIRST NAME OF BUDDY HOLLY'S FAMOUS LOVE SONG (E.G., "PEGGY SUE")

8. THEATER WHERE BUDDY HOLLY BROKE RACIAL BARRIERS BY PERFORMING

FATS DOMINO: THE NEW ORLEANS SOUND

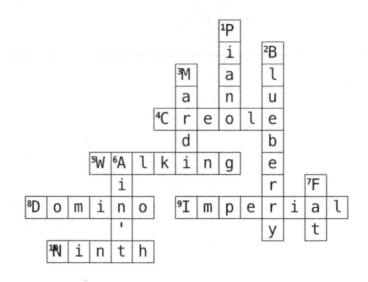

ACROSS

4. FATS DOMINO WAS A PART OF THIS CULTURAL GROUP FROM LOUISIANA

5. FATS DOMINO'S SONG THAT SAYS "I'M WALKING TO NEW ORLEANS"

8. FATS'S LAST NAME, WHICH BECAME HIS STAGE NAME

9. RECORD LABEL WHERE FATS DOMINO RELEASED MANY OF HIS HITS

10. THE WARD IN NEW ORLEANS WHERE FATS DOMINO GREW UP (AS IN "NINTH WARD")

DOWN

1. INSTRUMENT FATS DOMINO PLAYED IN A BOOGIE-WOOGIE STYLE

2. FIRST WORD OF A FATS DOMINO SONG ABOUT A HILL

3. FIRST WORD OF THE FAMOUS NEW ORLEANS FESTIVAL FATS OFTEN PLAYED (AS IN "MARDI GRAS")

6. FIRST WORD OF A FATS DOMINO SONG TITLED "AIN'T THAT A SHAME"

7. FIRST PART OF FATS DOMINO'S NICKNAME

LITTLE RICHARD: THE ARCHITECT OF ROCK

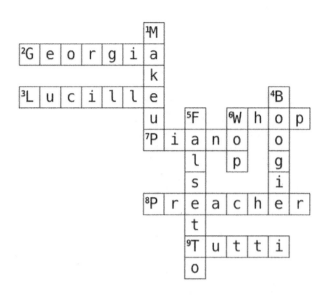

ACROSS

2. U.S. STATE WHERE LITTLE RICHARD WAS BORN

3. TITLE OF A LITTLE RICHARD HIT ABOUT A GIRL LEAVING HIM

6. ANOTHER REPEATED SYLLABLE IN "TUTTI FRUTTI" (THIRD PART OF "AWOPBOPALOOBOP")

7. INSTRUMENT LITTLE RICHARD PLAYED WITH FLAMBOYANT STYLE

8. LITTLE RICHARD'S OCCUPATION AFTER HE TEMPORARILY LEFT ROCK 'N' ROLL

9. FIRST WORD OF A LITTLE RICHARD HIT SONG WITH A LOT OF "AWOPBOPALOOBOP" ENERGY

DOWN

1. LITTLE RICHARD WAS KNOWN FOR WEARING THIS ON STAGE, BREAKING NORMS

4. DANCE STYLE LITTLE RICHARD HELPED POPULARIZE

5. VOCAL STYLE LITTLE RICHARD OFTEN USED IN HIS SINGING

6. REPEATED SYLLABLE IN "TUTTI FRUTTI" (SECOND PART OF "AWOPBOPALOOBOP")

TOP 10 HITS OF THE 1950S

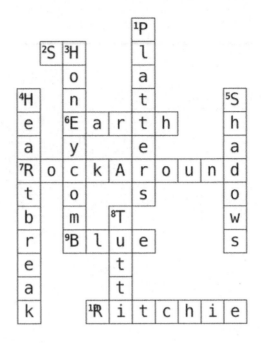

ACROSS

2. BOOM SONG BY THE CHORDS THAT IS CONSIDERED ONE OF THE FIRST ROCK 'N' ROLL HITS

6. FIRST WORD OF "GREAT BALLS OF FIRE" SINGER'S LAST NAME

7. FIRST TWO WORDS OF A HIT BY BILL HALEY & HIS COMETS (AS IN "ROCK AROUND THE CLOCK")

9. FIRST WORD OF ELVIS'S BALLAD ABOUT BEING

LONELY AT CHRISTMAS

10. FIRST NAME OF THE ARTIST WHO SANG "LA BAMBA"

DOWN

1. GROUP THAT SANG "THE GREAT PRETENDER"

3. SONG BY JIMMIE RODGERS THAT HIT #1 IN 1957

4. FIRST WORD OF ELVIS'S 1956 HIT ABOUT A HOTEL

5. LAST WORD OF "HEART AND SOUL" GROUP THE FOUR _____

8. FIRST WORD OF LITTLE RICHARD'S BREAKOUT HIT SONG

1960S ROCK ANTHEMS

ACROSS

2. FIRST WORD OF A DOORS SONG URGING YOU TO "LIGHT MY FIRE"

5. FIRST WORD OF JIMI HENDRIX'S SONG ABOUT A HAZE

6. ARETHA FRANKLIN'S ANTHEM DEMANDING THIS

9. FIRST WORD OF JIMI HENDRIX'S SONG WITH THE WORD "CHILD" IN THE TITLE

10. LAST WORD IN THE TITLE OF BOB DYLAN'S SONG "MR. _____ MAN"

DOWN

1. ICONIC ROLLING STONES SONG ABOUT NOT GETTING WHAT YOU WANT

3. BEATLES SONG THAT WAS ALSO THE TITLE OF A MOVIE

4. FIRST WORD OF "HOUSE OF THE RISING SUN" BY THE ANIMALS

7. LAST WORD OF A COLORFUL BEATLES SONG

8. FIRST WORD OF THE BEACH BOYS' HIT ABOUT GOOD VIBRATIONS

ROCK BALLADS: THE SOFTER SIDE

ACROSS

2. BEATLES' MOST COVERED BALLAD

3. FIRST WORD OF THE RIGHTEOUS BROTHERS' HIT ABOUT LOVE (AS IN "UNCHAINED MELODY")

5. FIRST WORD OF THE EVERLY BROTHERS' HIT ABOUT DREAMING

8. BEE GEES BALLAD THAT SAID "IT'S ONLY _____. AND WORDS ARE ALL I HAVE"

9. BEATLES SONG WITH A GIRL'S NAME AS THE TITLE

10. ROLLING STONES' BALLAD ABOUT A MYSTERIOUS WOMAN

DOWN

1. SONG BY THE BEATLES THAT'S BEEN COVERED BY OVER 2,200 ARTISTS

4. FIRST WORD OF THE SIMON & GARFUNKEL HIT "BRIDGE OVER TROUBLED WATER"

6. ROY ORBISON'S TEARFUL BALLAD

7. LAST WORD OF "WHAT KIND OF FOOL AM I" BY SAMMY DAVIS JR.

SONGS THAT SHAPED ROCK HISTORY

```
              ¹Z
          ²H  e  y
              p      ³H
              p      e      ⁴S
          ⁵B  e      r      t
          l   l      o      a
      ⁶I  m  a  g  i  n  e  s  i
          c      n      s      r
          k                     w
          ⁷B  o  ⁸H  e  m  i  a  n
          i      o             y
      ⁹B  r      t
  ¹F  l  o  y  d  e
          r      l
          n
```

DOWN

1. LAST WORD IN THE NAME OF THE BAND THAT SANG "WHOLE LOTTA LOVE" (AS IN "LED ZEPPELIN")

3. DAVID BOWIE'S ANTHEM ABOUT OVERCOMING THE ODDS

4. FIRST WORD OF A LED ZEPPELIN CLASSIC ABOUT A JOURNEY TO HEAVEN

5. BEATLES SONG ABOUT A BIRD WITH BROKEN WINGS

8. FIRST WORD OF AN EAGLES SONG ABOUT A CALIFORNIA ESTABLISHMENT

9. FIRST WORD OF A BRUCE SPRINGSTEEN HIT ABOUT LIFE IN THE USA

ACROSS

FIRST WORD OF THE BEATLES' SONG "HEY JDE"

JOHN LENNON'S SONG ABOUT PEACE AND JPE

FIRST WORD OF A QUEEN SONG WITH A HAPSODIC TITLE

. LAST WORD IN THE NAME OF THE BAND THAT ING "COMFORTABLY NUMB" (AS IN "PINK OYD")

41

DANCE CRAZE HITS

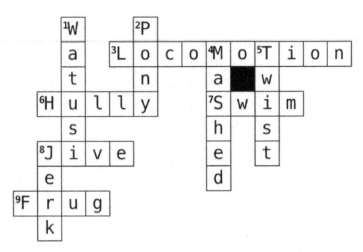

ACROSS

3. LITTLE EVA'S HIT SONG AND DANCE 6. FIRST WORD OF A DANCE BY THE OLYMPICS (AS IN "HULLY GULLY")

7. DANCE MOVE MENTIONED IN "SWIM" BY BOBBY FREEMAN

8. DANCE POPULARIZED IN THE 1950S, OFTEN DONE TO ROCK 'N' ROLL

9. DANCE MENTIONED IN THE SONG "THE FRUG" BY THE FRANTICS

DOWN

1. DANCE POPULARIZED BY THE ORLONS 2 DANCE MADE FAMOUS BY CHUBBY CHECKER AFTER "THE TWIST"

4. FIRST WORD OF A DANCE CRAZE NAME AFTER POTATOES (AS IN "MASHED POTATO")

5. DANCE MADE FAMOUS BY CHUBBY CHECKER

8. DANCE MENTIONED IN "THE JERK" BY TH LARKS

THE BEATLES

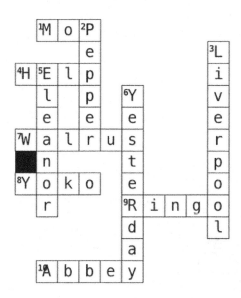

ACROSS

1. THE HAIRSTYLE FAMOUSLY ASSOCIATED WITH THE BEATLES (AS IN "MOP TOP")

4. BEATLES' SONG AND MOVIE TITLE ASKING FOR ASSISTANCE

7. ANIMAL REFERENCED IN THE BEATLES' SONG "I AM THE _____"

8. FIRST NAME OF JOHN LENNON'S WIFE

9. FIRST NAME OF THE BEATLES' DRUMMER

10. FIRST WORD OF THE BEATLES' FAMOUS STUDIO AND ALBUM (AS IN "ABBEY ROAD")

DOWN

2. FIRST WORD IN THE ALBUM TITLE "SGT. PEPPER'S LONELY HEARTS CLUB BAND"

3. THE BEATLES' HOMETOWN IN ENGLAND

5. FIRST NAME OF THE CHARACTER IN "ELEANOR RIGBY"

6. ONE-WORD TITLE OF A BEATLES BALLAD ABOUT NOSTALGIA

THE WHO: ROCK OPERA REVOLUTIONARIES

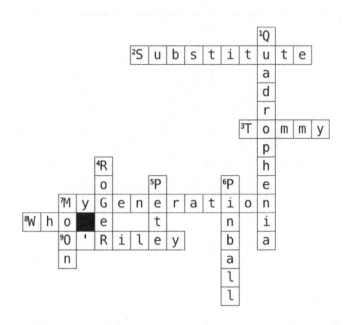

ACROSS

2. THE WHO'S SONG ABOUT BEING A REPLACEMENT

3. TITLE OF THE WHO'S ROCK OPERA ABOUT A DEAF, DUMB, AND BLIND BOY

7. THE WHO'S ANTHEM DECLARING "HOPE I DIE BEFORE I GET OLD" (TWO WORDS, ONE ANSWER)

8. BAND NAME FOLLOWED BY THE WORDS "ARE YOU" IN A FAMOUS SONG

9. LAST NAME REFERENCED IN "BABA O'RILEY" (COMMONLY MISTAKEN AS "TEENAGE WASTELAND")

DOWN

1. THE WHO'S ROCK OPERA ABOUT MODS AND ROCKERS

4. FIRST NAME OF THE WHO'S LEAD SINGER DALTREY

5. FIRST NAME OF THE WHO'S GUITARIST TOWNSHEND

6. GAME REFERENCED IN THE WHO'S "PINBALL WIZARD"

7. LAST NAME OF THE WHO'S DRUMMER KEITH

THE ROLLING STONES: ROCK'S BAD BOYS

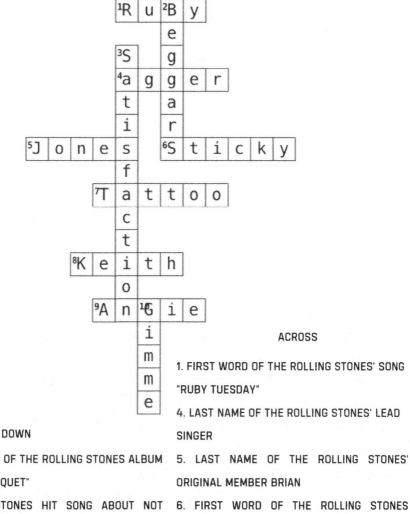

ACROSS

1. FIRST WORD OF THE ROLLING STONES' SONG "RUBY TUESDAY"

4. LAST NAME OF THE ROLLING STONES' LEAD SINGER

5. LAST NAME OF THE ROLLING STONES' ORIGINAL MEMBER BRIAN

6. FIRST WORD OF THE ROLLING STONES ALBUM "STICKY FINGERS"

7. FIRST WORD OF THE ALBUM TITLE "TATTOO YOU"

8. FIRST NAME OF THE ROLLING STONES' GUITARIST RICHARDS

9. ROLLING STONES BALLAD ABOUT A MYSTERIOUS WOMAN

DOWN

2. FIRST WORD OF THE ROLLING STONES ALBUM "BEGGARS BANQUET"

3. ROLLING STONES HIT SONG ABOUT NOT GETTING WHAT YOU WANT

10. FIRST WORD OF THE ROLLING STONES SONG ABOUT SHELTER

THE KINKS: THE BRITISH SOUND

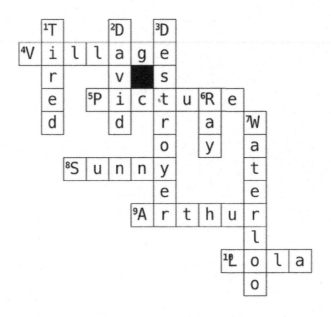

ACROSS

4. FIRST WORD OF THE KINKS' ALBUM "THE VILLAGE GREEN PRESERVATION SOCIETY"

5. FIRST WORD OF THE KINKS' SONG ABOUT PICTURES IN A GALLERY

8. FIRST WORD OF THE KINKS' SONG ABOUT A CERTAIN AFTERNOON

9. TITLE OF THE KINKS' ALBUM SUBTITLED "OR
THE DECLINE AND FALL OF THE BRITISH EMPIRE"

10. THE KINKS' SONG ABOUT A GIRL WHO ISN'T
QUITE WHAT SHE SEEMS

DOWN

1. FIRST WORD OF THE KINKS' HIT ABOUT BEING "TIRED OF WAITING FOR YOU"

2. LAST NAME OF THE KINKS' CO-FOUNDER AND GUITARIST DAVE

3. THE KINKS SONG WHERE LOLA REAPPEARS

6. FIRST NAME OF THE KINKS' LEAD SINGER DAVIES

7. FIRST WORD OF THE KINKS' HIT SONG ABOUT A SUNSET

THE YARDBIRDS AND BEYOND: GUITAR GODS

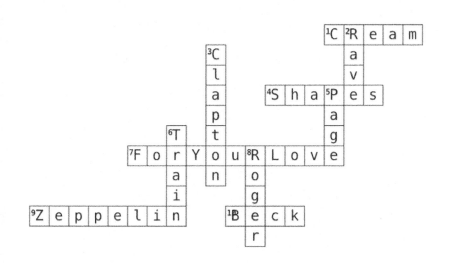

<table>
<tr><td></td><td></td><td></td><td></td><td></td><td></td><td></td><td>¹C</td><td>²R</td><td>e</td><td>a</td><td>m</td></tr>
<tr><td></td><td></td><td>³C</td><td></td><td></td><td></td><td></td><td></td><td>a</td></tr>
</table>

	ACROSS		DOWN

<table border="1">
<tr>
<td colspan="2" align="center">ACROSS</td>
<td colspan="2" align="center">DOWN</td>
</tr>
</table>

ACROSS

BAND CLAPTON FORMED AFTER LEAVING THE YARDBIRDS

FIRST WORD OF THE YARDBIRDS' HIT SONG "SHAPES OF THINGS"

YARDBIRDS' HIT SONG THAT CLAPTON DISLIKED (THREE WORDS, ONE ANSWER)

LAST NAME OF THE BAND PAGE FORMED AFTER THE YARDBIRDS (AS IN "LED ZEPPELIN")

. LAST NAME OF THE GUITARIST WHO FOLLOWED CLAPTON IN THE YARDBIRDS

DOWN

2. FIRST WORD OF THE YARDBIRDS' ALBUM "RAVE UP"

3. LAST NAME OF THE GUITARIST NICKNAMED "SLOWHAND"

5. LAST NAME OF THE GUITARIST WHO LATER FORMED LED ZEPPELIN

6. FIRST WORD OF THE YARDBIRDS' SONG "TRAIN KEPT A-ROLLIN'"

8. FIRST NAME OF THE YARDBIRDS' BASSIST MCCARTY

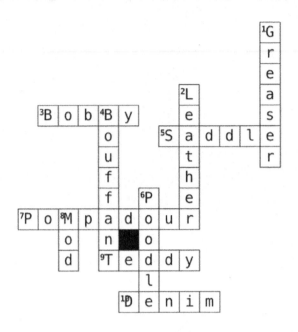

ACROSS

3. TYPE OF SOCKS POPULAR IN THE 1950S ROCK 'N' ROLL ERA

5. TYPE OF SHOE WITH A THICK SOLE AND LOW HEEL, POPULAR IN THE 1950S

7. HAIRSTYLE MADE FAMOUS BY ELVIS PRESLEY

9. BRITISH YOUTH SUBCULTURE KNOWN FOR THEIR DRAPE JACKETS AND ROCK 'N' ROLL STYLE (AS IN "TEDDY BOYS")

10. FABRIC ASSOCIATED WITH ROCK 'N' ROLL FASHION, ESPECIALLY JEANS

DOWN

1. TERM FOR THE LEATHER JACKET-WEARING ROCK 'N' ROLL REBELS OF THE 1950S

2. MATERIAL ASSOCIATED WITH THE REBELLIOUS ROCK 'N' ROLL LOOK

4. VOLUMINOUS HAIRSTYLE POPULAR AMONG WOMEN IN THE 1960S

6. TYPE OF SKIRT THAT BECAME A SYMBOL OF 1950S ROCK 'N' ROLL FASHION

8. 1960S BRITISH SUBCULTURE KNOWN FOR ITS SHARP FASHION AND LOVE OF ROCK 'N' ROLL

ROCK 'N' ROLL HALL OF FAME: THE EARLY INDUCTEES

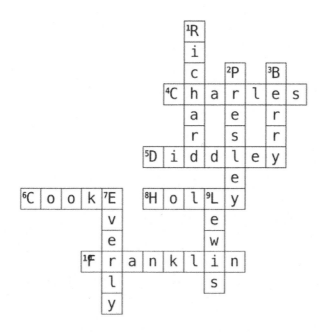

ACROSS

4. LAST NAME OF THE SINGER AND PIANIST KNOWN FOR BLENDING SOUL AND ROCK 'N' ROLL

5. LAST NAME OF THE ROCK 'N' ROLL INNOVATOR KNOWN FOR HIS DISTINCTIVE BEAT AND GUITAR STYLE

6. LAST NAME OF THE SINGER KNOWN FOR "YOU SEND ME" AND A KEY FIGURE IN THE DEVELOPMENT OF SOUL AND ROCK 8. LAST NAME OF THE "PEGGY SUE" SINGER INDUCTED IN 1986

10. LAST NAME OF THE "QUEEN OF SOUL" WHO WAS ALSO AN EARLY INDUCTEE

DOWN

1. LAST NAME OF "TUTTI FRUTTI" ROCK 'N' ROLL PIONEER INDUCTED EARLY

2. FIRST INDUCTEE INTO THE ROCK 'N' ROLL HALL OF FAME

3. LAST NAME OF THE "ROLL OVER BEETHOVEN" SINGER INDUCTED INTO THE HALL OF FAME

7. LAST NAME OF THE BROTHERS WHO WERE EARLY INDUCTEES

9. LAST NAME OF THE "GREAT BALLS OF FIRE" SINGER INDUCTED INTO THE HALL OF FAME

TV SHOWS AND ROCK PERFORMANCES

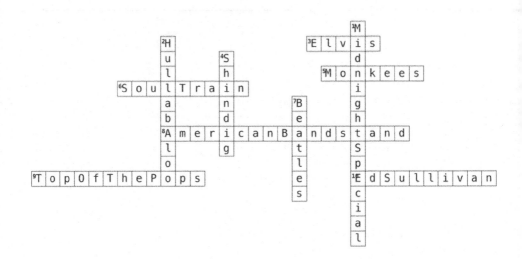

ACROSS

3. ROCK 'N' ROLL STAR WHO FAMOUSLY APPEARED ON "THE ED SULLIVAN SHOW" IN 1956

5. TV SHOW ABOUT A FICTIONAL ROCK BAND, LEADING TO REAL CHART-TOPPING HITS

6. TV SHOW THAT, WHILE FOCUSED ON SOUL, ALSO FEATURED ROCK 'N' ROLL CROSSOVERS (TWO WORDS, ONE ANSWER)

8. POPULAR TV SHOW HOSTED BY DICK CLARK THAT FEATURED ROCK 'N' ROLL ACTS (TWO WORDS, ONE ANSWER)

9. BRITISH TV SHOW THAT SHOWCASED ROCK 'N' ROLL HITS (THREE WORDS, ONE ANSWER)

10. TV SHOW WHERE THE BEATLES MADE THEIR U.S. DEBUT (TWO WORDS, ONE ANSWER)

DOWN

1. 1970S TV SHOW THAT FEATURED LIVE ROCK PERFORMANCES (TWO WORDS, ONE ANSWER)

2. 1960S NBC TV SHOW KNOWN FOR SHOWCASING ROCK 'N' ROLL STARS

4. 1960S AMERICAN MUSIC TV SHOW THAT FEATURED ROCK 'N' ROLL PERFORMANCES

7. BAND THAT CAUSED "BEATLEMANIA" AFTER THEIR ED SULLIVAN PERFORMANCE

ROCK 'N' ROLL MOVIES: THE SOUNDTRACKS OF A GENERATION

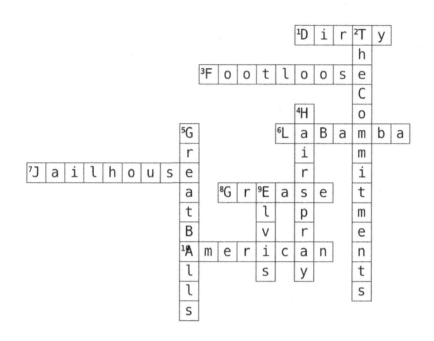

ACROSS

1. FIRST WORD OF THE TITLE "DIRTY DANCING," SET IN THE 1960S

3. 1984 MOVIE ABOUT A TOWN THAT BANS DANCING

6. MOVIE ABOUT THE LIFE OF RITCHIE VALENS (TWO WORDS, ONE ANSWER)

7. FIRST WORD OF THE ELVIS MOVIE AND SONG "JAILHOUSE ROCK"

8. 1978 MOVIE FEATURING A 1950S ROCK 'N' ROLL HIGH SCHOOL SETTING

10. FIRST WORD OF "AMERICAN GRAFFITI," A FILM SET IN THE EARLY 1960S

DOWN

2. MOVIE ABOUT AN IRISH SOUL BAND COVERING (60S HITS (TWO WORDS, ONE ANSWER)

4. MOVIE ABOUT A DANCE SHOW AND CIVIL RIGHTS SET IN THE 1960S

5. FIRST TWO WORDS OF THE JERRY LEE LEWIS BIOPIC TITLE (AS IN "GREAT BALLS OF FIRE!")

9. ROCK 'N' ROLL STAR WHO HAD A SUCCESSFUL FILM CAREER IN THE 1950S AND 1960S

ROCK 'N' ROLL IN ADVERTISING: THE SOUND OF SALES

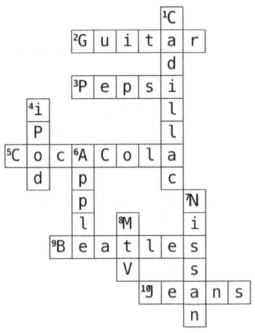

ACROSS

2. INSTRUMENT OFTEN FEATURED IN ADS FOR ROCK 'N' ROLL-THEMED PRODUCTS

3. SOFT DRINK COMPANY THAT FAMOUSLY USED ROCK MUSIC IN ITS MARKETING, INCLUDING MICHAEL JACKSON

5. BEVERAGE COMPANY KNOWN FOR USING ROCK 'N' ROLL MUSIC IN THEIR ADS (TWO WORDS, ONE ANSWER)

9. BAND WHOSE SONG "REVOLUTION" WAS USED IN A NIKE COMMERCIAL

10. FASHION ITEM OFTEN SOLD USING ROCK 'N' ROLL IMAGERY AND MUSIC

DOWN

1. CAR BRAND THAT USED LED ZEPPELIN'S "ROCK AND ROLL" IN COMMERCIALS

4. APPLE PRODUCT THAT FEATURED VARIOUS ROCK 'N' ROLL SONGS IN ITS ADS

6. COMPANY THAT USED U2'S SONG "VERTIGO" IN AN AD CAMPAIGN

7. CAR COMPANY THAT USED THE WHO'S "BABA O'RILEY" IN A COMMERCIAL

8. NETWORK THAT REVOLUTIONIZED MUSIC ADVERTISING WITH ROCK 'N' ROLL MUSIC VIDEOS

SURVIVORS OF ROCK: ARTISTS WHO ENDURED

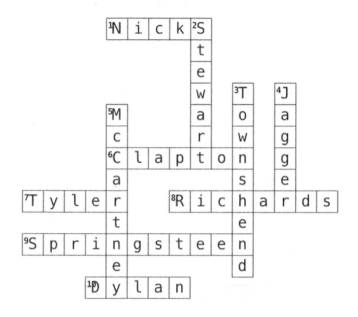

ACROSS

LAST NAME OF THE FLEETWOOD MAC SINGER TILL PERFORMING SOLO AND WITH THE BAND

LAST NAME OF THE GUITARIST KNOWN AS "SLOWHAND," WHO HAS HAD A LONG CAREER

LAST NAME OF THE AEROSMITH FRONTMAN KNOWN FOR HIS ENERGETIC PERFORMANCES

LAST NAME OF THE ROLLING STONES' GUITARIST KNOWN FOR HIS RESILIENCE

LAST NAME OF "THE BOSS" WHO IS FAMOUS FOR HIS LONG CONCERTS

LAST NAME OF THE FOLK-ROCK ICON STILL ACTIVE AFTER SIX DECADES

DOWN

2. LAST NAME OF THE RASPY-VOICED ROCKER KNOWN FOR "MAGGIE MAY"

3. LAST NAME OF THE WHO'S GUITARIST WHO HELPED PIONEER ROCK OPERAS

4. LAST NAME OF THE ROLLING STONES' LEAD SINGER WHO STILL TOURS

5. LAST NAME OF THE BEATLE WHO CONTINUES TO PERFORM GLOBALLY

REUNIONS AND COMEBACKS: ROCK'S GREATEST RETURNS

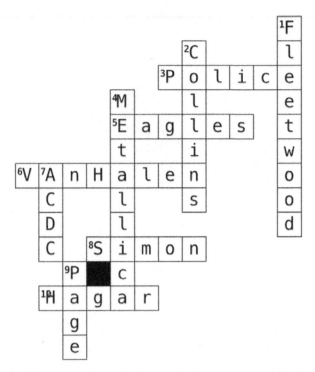

ACROSS

3. BAND THAT REUNITED IN 2007 FOR A WORLD
TOUR AFTER DECADES APART
5. BAND THAT FAMOUSLY SAID "HELL FREEZES OVER" AND THEN REUNITED
6. BAND THAT REUNITED WITH DAVID LEE ROTH
FOR TOURS IN THE 2000S
8. LAST NAME OF THE "BRIDGE OVER TROUBLED
WATER" SINGER WHO REUNITED WITH GARFUNKEL
10. LAST NAME OF THE "RED ROCKER" WHO REJOINED VAN HALEN IN 2004

DOWN

1. LAST NAME OF THE DRUMMER WHOSE BAND REUNITED FOR "THE DANCE"
2. LAST NAME OF THE GENESIS DRUMMER AND SINGER WHO RETURNED FOR A 2007 TOUR
4. BAND THAT HAS HAD MULTIPLE REUNIONS AND LINE-UP CHANGES, STAYING STRONG
7. BAND KNOWN FOR SURVIVING THE DEATH OF ITS LEAD SINGER AND COMING BACK STRONGER
9. LAST NAME OF THE LED ZEPPELIN GUITARIST WHO REUNITED WITH THE BAND IN 2007

ROCK 'N' ROLL'S ENDURING INFLUENCE: FROM THEN TO NOW

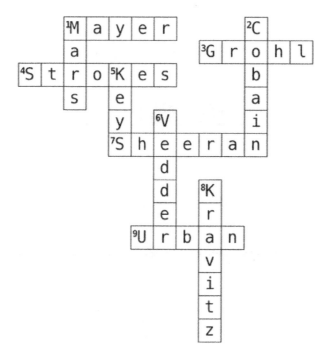

ACROSS

1. LAST NAME OF THE GUITARIST AND SINGER WHO DRAWS HEAVILY FROM BLUES-ROCK

3. LAST NAME OF THE FOO FIGHTERS FRONTMAN WHO STARTED AS NIRVANA'S DRUMMER

4. BAND THAT BROUGHT BACK GARAGE ROCK IN THE EARLY 2000S, INSPIRED BY THE 1970S

7. LAST NAME OF THE BRITISH SINGER-SONGWRITER WHO OFTEN COVERS CLASSIC ROCK SONGS

9. LAST NAME OF THE COUNTRY SINGER WHO INCORPORATES ROCK INTO HIS MUSIC

DOWN

1. LAST NAME OF THE POP STAR WHO CHANNELS ROCK, FUNK, AND SOUL IN HIS PERFORMANCES

2. LAST NAME OF THE NIRVANA FRONTMAN WHO CITED THE BEATLES AS AN INFLUENCE

5. LAST NAME OF THE SINGER ALICIA, WHO WAS INFLUENCED BY SOUL AND ROCK

6. LAST NAME OF THE PEARL JAM SINGER INFLUENCED BY THE WHO

8. LAST NAME OF THE SINGER WHO BLENDS ROCK, FUNK, AND SOUL INFLUENCES

COVER VERSIONS: NEW TAKES ON CLASSIC HITS

ACROSS

3. LAST NAME OF THE SINGER WHO COVERED "VALERIE," MAKING IT A HIT

4. LAST NAME OF THE SINGER WHO MADE "ME AND BOBBY MCGEE" FAMOUS

5. LAST NAME OF THE GUITARIST WHO FAMOUSLY COVERED "ALL ALONG THE WATCHTOWER"

6. BAND THAT COVERED "CALIFORNIA SUN" AND BROUGHT PUNK TO THE MASSES

8. LAST NAME OF THE COUNTRY ICON WHO COVERED NINE INCH NAILS' "HURT"

DOWN

1. LAST NAME OF THE ARTIST WHO COVERED "BLUE SUEDE SHOES"

2. LAST NAME OF THE GUITARIST WHO COVERED "I SHOT THE SHERIFF"

3. LAST NAME OF THE WHITE STRIPES FRONTMAN WHO COVERED "JOLENE"

7. LAST NAME OF THE SINGER WHO COVERED "BECAUSE THE NIGHT" AND CO-WROTE IT WITH SPRINGSTEEN

8. LAST NAME OF THE SINGER WHO FAMOUSLY COVERED "WITH A LITTLE HELP FROM MY FRIENDS"

THE DAY THE MUSIC DIED: REMEMBERING THE LOST LEGENDS

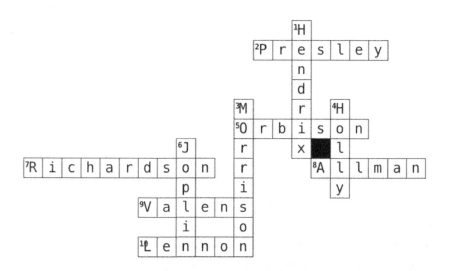

ACROSS

2. LAST NAME OF "THE KING" WHO PASSED AWAY IN 1977

5. LAST NAME OF THE "OH, PRETTY WOMAN" SINGER WHO PASSED IN 1988

7. LAST NAME OF "THE BIG BOPPER," WHO WAS ON THE SAME ILL-FATED FLIGHT

8. LAST NAME OF THE GUITARIST FROM THE ALLMAN BROTHERS BAND WHO DIED IN 1971

9. LAST NAME OF THE "LA BAMBA" SINGER WHO ALSO PERISHED IN THE CRASH

10. LAST NAME OF THE FORMER BEATLE TRAGICALLY KILLED IN 1980

DOWN

1. LAST NAME OF THE LEGENDARY GUITARIST WHO ALSO DIED AT AGE 27

3. LAST NAME OF THE DOORS' LEAD SINGER WHO DIED AT AGE 27

4. LAST NAME OF THE SINGER WHO DIED IN A 1959 PLANE CRASH, KNOWN FOR "PEGGY SUE"

6. LAST NAME OF THE "PIECE OF MY HEART" SINGER WHO DIED IN 1970

ENJOYED SOLVING THESE CROSSWORDS? WE'D LOVE TO HEAR
YOUR THOUGHTS—PLEASE LEAVE A REVIEW AND LET US KNOW
HOW WE DID!

@MOLLYMCMANUS

Made in United States
Orlando, FL
16 December 2024

55922723R00036